# THE BOOK OF HOURS

FRIDA ESCOBEDO

TEXTS BY

MARÍA GÓMEZ DE LEÓN LÓPEZ

PHOTOS BY

ANA GÓMEZ DE LEÓN LÓPEZ

As social life becomes utterly secularized, spaces for contemplation are becoming increasingly scarce. Workspaces and households have been optimized to efficiently meet our bodily needs but lack a consecrated space in which we can bracket the outside world for a considerable amount of time to introspect. Indeed, contemplation calls for four elements: space and time, a subject and an object. In antiquity, shrines and museums provided people with the first. They served as public spaces with a highly private purpose, to turn the mind's eye inwardly, chiefly through the contemplation of objects. Icons, domes, symbols. Pilgrims traveled across lands to commune with these entities. Progressively, however, as literacy increased, people turned towards a more personal devotional practice, which stood in opposition to the liturgy. Soon, a smaller kind of shrine made its way to the people in the form of personal books.



Perhaps as ubiquitous as smartphones today, books of hours were almost a private necessity in Europe during the Middle Ages. Within their pages, they carried collections of texts that were meaningful to their owners, as well as an organized way of structuring the day around prayer, marking the passing of the canonical hours. All books of hours contained sections to be recited at regular intervals throughout the twenty-four hours of the day. Many included a calendar and a cycle of prayer devoted to the Virgin Mary. And yet, no two books were alike. Some were luxuriously sized as modern-day art books, while others were tiny enough to be worn as jewelry. Highly personalized, with intricate miniatures and illuminations, the books of hours were extremely popular. When the invention of printing made them even more widely available, people still preferred the handmade versions perhaps because of the ways in which their designs encapsulated hours of miniature labor. In them, the public and the private timescales converged, crystalized into a material, perdurable form not devoid of beauty.

The present *Book of Hours* is a modern exegesis of that extinct devotional practice: a project in which twenty-four objects were photographed at different intervals of time to capture their evolution, making a new calendar of matter and light. As humanity has transitioned to a secular understanding of time in which hours are organized and conceived in terms of productivity, this *Book of Hours* interrogates the place of contemplation in our era, its possibilities and challenges. Throughout this book – a public display of a private collection of objects – readers are invited to contemplate these arrays of matter, and experience the ways in which they once interacted with light, that bright needle in time's fabric.

In sharp opposition to the highly structured, dutiful ethos of the book of hours, this particular articulation of the genre calls for an investigation of a private collection of objects, belonging to Frida Escobedo. And what is a private collection if not an urge against duty? There is more than one way in which the collector of objects is a rebel. A person who collects resists the human urge to consume, to categorize things in terms of their utility. Collections hold a relationship to their objects which does not emphasize their functional, utilitarian value. All collected objects are therefore decontextualized, shorn from their environment, but not altogether devoid of their histories, which have already previously informed them. It is precisely because collected objects are decontextualized that they can be better contemplated. We sense them fully. All noise is bracketed. The white background or the clear glass of the cabinet function as a blank slate, but also, according to Walter Benjamin, "everything remembered and thought, everything conscious, becomes the pedestal, the frame, the base, the lock of [the collector's] property."

Because personal collections, such as the one presented in this book, are thus intimate and silent, they may appear to be quite arbitrary. When I was commissioned to write 24 texts responding to the 24 objects in this collection, I soon understood I would never access their true value. There is a secret value these objects hold for their collector, my sister. I find this mystery, this obscure inaccessibility, very exciting. I can only hope the reader does too.

At times, I felt the urge to include some of the wonderful stories behind these objects. A group of blue porcelain shards, for instance, was found by my sister at the shores of the Tohoku region in Japan. These fragments were stranded on a beach that seemed virgin at first sight, but concealed in its natural semblance a recent past, a tsunami that had devastated the region in 2011, destroying hundreds of households. Months after the disaster, my sister found pieces of broken tableware along the shore: a testimony of the precarious divide between what is natural and what is artificial, a new and terrifying definition of ruin. I decided, however, to not contextualize the objects and let them shine on their own. In the same way that in the books of hours the images did not directly illustrate the text, here too the images were but tipping points for me to weave another parallel collection of fragments.

Hence, *The Book of Hours* is at once a collection of objects and a collection of texts. The book is transformed not only into a portable cabinet of curiosities but into a portable library. A circadian clock of words and references. In order to honor the serendipity of the objects in the collection and the original idea of the book of hours, I have attached texts that at first seem randomly *found*. Only when considered as a whole do they cohere. I have included lines of poetry, scientific articles, lyrics and philosophical texts I treasure and which I have found and gleaned for years. Because more often than not my own poems seem to me to be found objects too, I have included a few. At times, I have intervened in others' poems, a practice called erasure, in which parts of an original text are omitted to uncover another hidden text. To me, this mimics the erosion that has slowly shaped many of the objects in this book. I like to think texts are subject to erosion too, they are mutable and can change meaning depending on our focus and exegesis, depending on which parts are illuminated and which words are obscured.

The idea of erasure came directly from the photographs I received. My sister Ana Gómez de León beautifully captured the way these objects interact with light, but also how they interact with shadows. Moreover, I realized the objects *produced* and projected their own shadows. "All objects are natural sundials, so outdoor shadows contain clues about the time (given the place) and the place (given the time)", writes Roy Sorensen. This is exactly the concept behind this book. Because of shadows and light, the more we lose information about place the more we gain information about time, and the less we know about time, the more we know about place.

If I had to believe there is holiness in this world, I would say it is contained in books and stones. Books are a special type of place that holds time: I see one of the shelves in my bookcase and I can see cubic meters of paper, for sure, but there are months or years contained inside. And, in fact, stones are a special kind of book, a foliated record of history. Rocks are a special kind of clock; they are the clocks of a time we cannot access. As humans, we are excluded from the experience of deep time, the geological time that is recorded like scripture in the accumulating layers of sediment.

Likewise, we are deprived of deep time's logical counterpoint: the moment. Photography is the only tool that has allowed us to come closer to the alchemical, ever unattainable present moment. Today, the fastest shutter speed is 1/8000 of a second. The photographs in this book taken together do not amount to even one second. They are tokens of an infinitesimally minute present, not perceivable to us humans without technology. We invite readers to contemplate these records of split seconds for hours. To contemplate the books of stones for minutes. Our project is to make the present expansible, and uncover the deep abysses that every single object truly has inside.

One last thing should be said about the objects in this series. Most of them were not made by anyone. They simply came to be. This is perhaps the biggest gap between the medieval books of hours and our reinterpretation of them. If both are invitations to contemplation and devotion, in the latter the natural world is taken as the work of a master. In our secular times, we question the notion of the world as creation. We believe there is still a beauty to that. These objects won a battle against randomness and chance. "For what else is this collection but a disorder to which habit has accommodated itself to such an extent that it can appear as order?", inquired Benjamin, as he organized his library. Collections as manifestations of chaos that can appear as order. What could be more similar to a religion? The urge to organize a seemingly random, teeming natural world under the broad categories of creation. By virtue of this project we seek to highlight the active and productive forces of contemplation.

Why else would stones, nestled deep into the caves of Earth, have colors patterns and luster that can only be appreciated with light? How can we imagine a modern-day revelation?

One proviso: too much light can be disorienting. Legend says that in the *Krak des Chevaliers* (Castle of Knights) in Syria a passageway was built so that when people crossed its long stretch of darkness and then reached the castle esplanade, they were exposed suddenly and violently into broad daylight. This architectural feature was meant to dazzle invaders (Sorensen 7). There can be no revelation without holding mystery. There can be no orientation through light without objects, and the absence of light they leave behind.

P. 008 Fig. 01 07:11 H

Therefore, we should not say that one man's hour is worth another man's hour, but rather that one man during an hour is worth just as much as another man during an hour. Time is everything, man is nothing; he is at the most the incarnation of time. (Marx, 1867)

P. 010 Fig. 02 07:20 H

Husk, and the trees are all in labor.
Come fire, come hail, a book is readily open.
One poet wrote, *the trees give birth so far*
*away from themselves*. Wanting elsewhere
to begin. Each leaf an hour long,
seasons away from here, here
is a place to begin with, almost
visible.
(After Valeria List)

P. 012 Fig. 03 07:25 H

As labor is progressively rationalized and mechanized activity becomes less and less active and more and more contemplative. The contemplative stance adopted towards a process mechanically conforming to fixed laws reduces space and time to a common denominator and degrades time to the dimension of space. (Lukács, 1923)

P. 014 Fig. 04 07:38 H

One blue, massive wind
blows like a see-through fire
against her. And the waves
flowing in all possible directions,
like song, cancel each other out.
The Zephyr erodes first
her eyelids, splits the ends
of the seconds of her mane,
her shadow falls like another wind
against the wind. Hours, with the red?
dye of your empty fabric, do you
protect or cover, do you hide?
(After Sandro Botticelli's "Birth of Venus")

P. 016    Fig. 05

07:40 H

I travel from land,
said trunkless stone
in the desert the sand
Half sunk a
lip of cold

Which survive s these lifeless things,
The hand that the heart fed
on these words :
My name is
Work
Nothing remains
Of that ,
sands stretch away
(Shelley, "Ozymandias", 1818)

P. 020 Fig. 07 08:38 H

the most essential part of a living cell – the chromosome fibre – may suitably be called an aperiodic crystal. In physics we have dealt hitherto only with periodic crystals. To a humble physicist's mind, these are very interesting and complicated objects; they constitute one of the most fascinating and complex material structures by which inanimate nature puzzles his wits. Yet, compared with the aperiodic crystal, they are rather plain and dull. The difference in structure is of the same kind as that between an ordinary wallpaper in which the same pattern is repeated again and again in regular periodicity and a masterpiece of embroidery, say a Raphael tapestry, which shows no dull repetition, but an elaborate, coherent, meaningful design traced by the great master. (Schrödinger, "What is Life?", 1944)

P. 022 Fig. 08 09:08 H

She sang

Like

empty sleeves

,

we understood

the ocean.

sea was a mask

we

heard,

in all her

wind;

But

the maker

walked to

ask

the dark

by many waves

If

speech

was more than

ours among

high atmospheres

It was

measured to the hour

of the world

That was her song,

there never was a world

made.

if

the singing ended

, the glass

portioned out the

zones

Arranging night.

rage for order

rage to order sea

Words portals

sound

(Stevens, "The Idea of Order at Key West", 1934)

P. 024 Fig. 09 09:12 H

Non-being or absence is not in the usual case meant to be pure nothing. It is the absence or non-existence of some entity or entities that is quite compatible with the presence of existence of other entities at the same place and time. Non-being is not a form of being any more than being is a form of non-being. Yet the fittings, the warp and woof of the presence and absence of something are essential and complementary for one another. Indeed, the concept of an edge is a concept of the limit of where something is and where something isn't. Presences and absences are correlative and both are involved in destroying, removing and being at a distance from things. (Martin, 1996)

P. 026 Fig. 10 09:14 H

Slower, held, if the backbeat,
where the future is not here. If
when. A taxidermy of wind.

P. 028 Fig. 11 09:16 H

My looking ripens things. (Rilke, 1905)

P. 030 Fig. 12 09:51 H

You can take the bark away from the tree, and the nerves
from the leaf, you can remove the years from the heartwood,
take the sapwood from the sap, you can remove the milk
from the blood and separate the sound from wind, and you
can distill the body from the mind, no dregs remain, the bark
excised from the dog at night, the tree giving up its dual breath.
You can peel the health off from the wound, encase the fragrance
of the hours, but you cannot rinse that smell from your eyes.

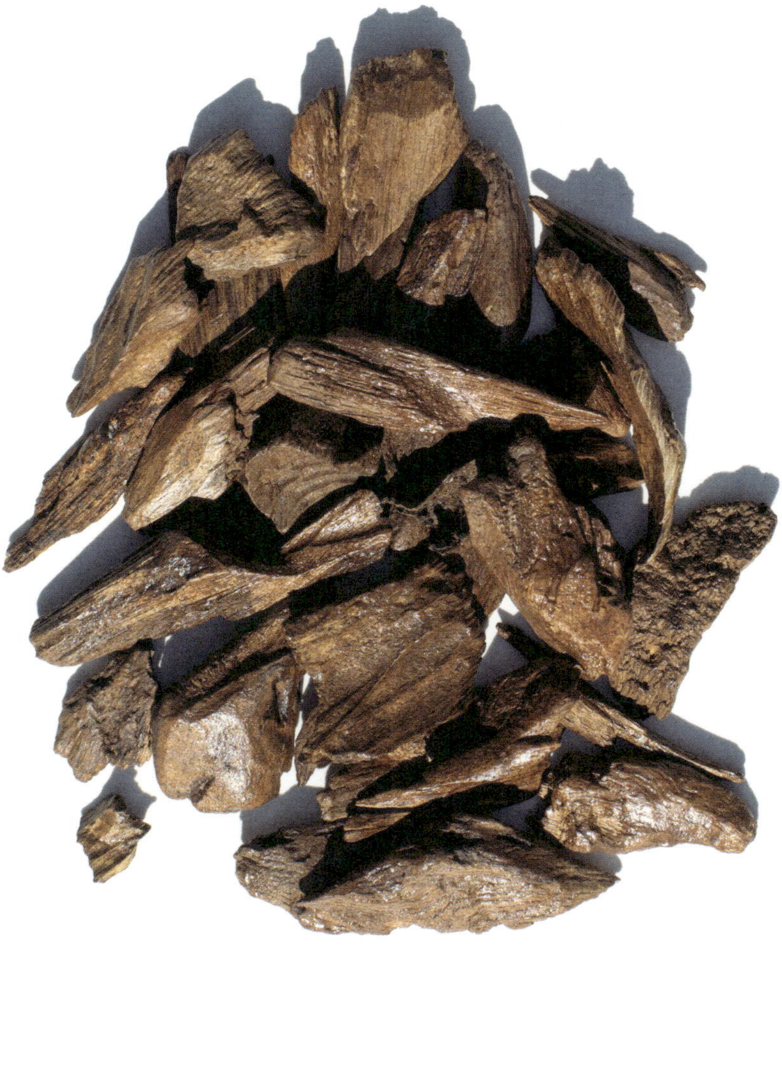

P. 032 Fig. 13 10:03 H

Stones, like us, stand at the intersection of countless lines crossing one another and receding to infinity, at the center of a field of forces too unpredictable to be measured; and we awkwardly call the result chance, hazard, or fate (Yourcenar, 1985)

P. 034     Fig. 14                                    10:12 H

If time stood very still, could I be the worker?
Timestamp: I work my beauty into winter.
Timestamp: winter burns my wings, still
    I manufacture silence.
Timestamp: from ahead the trees quicken, stall,
    and I can see the wide shoulders of the Earth, the
    white sea, grass awakening
    to pink noise, listen to the plastic
    wrapper of the rain
Timestamp: one first foot on earth, a drop, a swarm,
    the rain is learning how to walk
Timestamp: Beads of resin in my voice,
    but the rain outruns me.

P. 036 Fig. 15 10:19 H

I live my life in widening circles
that reach out across the world.
I may not complete this last one
but I give myself to it. (Rilke, 1905)

P. 038 Fig. 16 10:53 H

And the meteorite's just what causes the light
And the meteor's how it's perceived
And the meteoroid's a bone thrown from the void that lies quiet in offering to thee
(Newsom, 2006)

P. 040 Fig. 17 11:00 H

P. 042 Fig. 18 14:14 H

Doctor, I have a pain in my finger: I place
my finger in my mouth:
I have a pain in my mouth.

Subject, there is nothing in the box:
The box is in the universe: There
is: nothing in the universe.

P. 044 Fig. 19 15:37 H

For a stone represents an obvious achievement, yet one arrived at without invention, skill, industry, or anything else that would make it a work in the human sense of the word, much less a work of art (Caillois, 1985)

P. 046　Fig. 20　16:01 H

(1) Anything that is occupying a space just its own size is at rest.
(2) A moving arrow, while it is moving, is moving in the present.
(3) But in the present the arrow is occupying a space just its own size.
(4) Therefore, in the present the arrow is at rest.
(5) Therefore, the moving arrow, while it is moving, is at rest.

(Zeno reconstructed by Lear, 1981)

P. 048 Fig. 21 18:07 H

film to gold to avalanche to yeast infection
to solar wind to palm to tap water to redshift
to pearl to krummholz to nuclear
waste to bread to saffron to bulbs to missionary
to omicron to turnstile to cold snap to lithium
to storm to birthday tulips to tape to
blackboard to canoe to sandalwood to cedar
fever to aerosol to white water to cloth-
bound to beeswax to gulf to barbwire
to June to limelight to

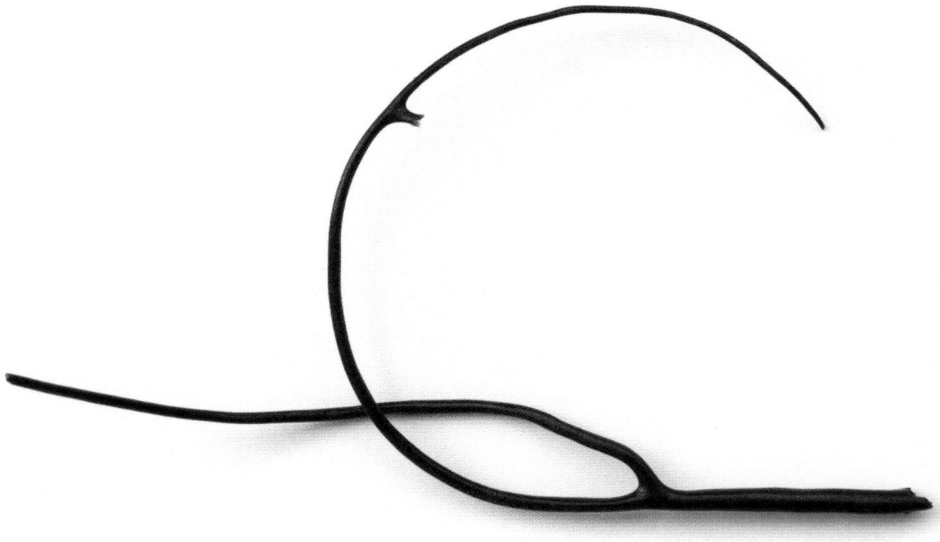

P. 050 Fig. 22 18:30 H

2 x 2 x 2 cm

P. 052 Fig. 23 18:53 H

Nothingness was like a wound to you,
You cooled it with the world.

Now it heals quietly among us. (Rilke, 1905)

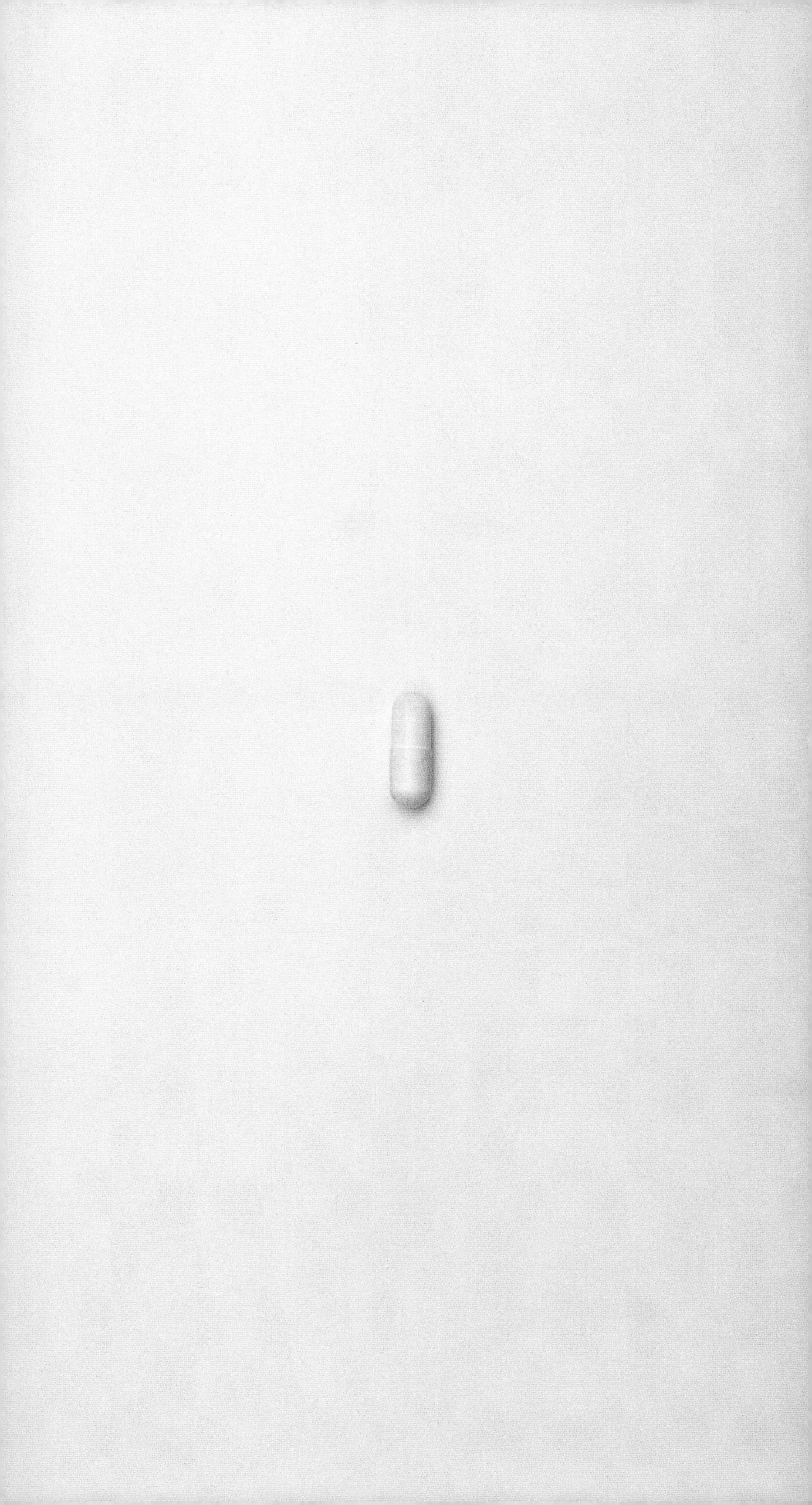

P. 054 Fig. 24 19:30 H

That inside the cave there was an organ of light.
That there was no light but it already had a vessel.
That the mountain, too, it had a dome, but several
seasons covered it, covered.
That the skull had a window midday.
That the skull dreamt of aquamarines growing underneath.
That the mountain had a thought it could not remember.
There is a shadow of day and a shadow of night
installed at the center of the body.
There is a dream of day and a dream of night
inside the night. A second blood, ticking, circadian.

P. 006 Benjamin, Walter. "Unpacking my Library." *Illuminations: Essays and Reflections*, edited by Hannah Arendt. Translated by Harry Zohn. Fontana Collins, 1970.

P. 007 Sorensen, Roy A. *Seeing Dark Things: The Philosophy of Shadows*, New York: Oxford University Press, 2008.

P. 008 Marx, Karl. *The Poverty of Philosophy*. Moscow: Foreign Languages Pub. House, 1955.

P. 012 Lukács, György. *History and Class Consciousness*. Translated by Rodney Livingstone. Cambridge, Mass: MIT Press, 1971.

P. 016 Corcoran, Patricia. Photograph. *Plastic Permanence: Our Litter Is Now Part of the Geologic Record* by Kathryn Potraz. Sierra Club, 22 July 2014, www.sierraclub.org/sierra/2014-4-july-august/green-life/plastic-permanence-our-litter-now-part-geologic-record.

P. 018 Shelley, Percy Bysshe. "Ozymandias." *Poetry Foundation*, 2017, www.poetryfoundation.org/poems/46565/ozymandias.

P. 020 Schrödinger, Erwin. *What Is Life? and Other Scientific Essays*. Garden City: Doubleday, 1956.

P. 022 Stevens, Wallace. "The Idea of Order at Key West." *The Collected Poems of Wallace Stevens*, New York: Alfred A. Knopf, 1977.

P. 024 Martin, C. B. "How It Is: Entities, Absences and Voids." *Australasian Journal of Philosophy* 74.1 (1996): pp. 57-65. WeNewsom, Joanna, and Van Dyke, Parks. "Ys Joanna Newsom." Drag City, 2006. Television.

PP. 028
036
052 Rilke, Rainer Maria. *The Book of Hours: Prayers to a Lowly God.* Translated by Annemarie S. Kidder. Evanston: Northwestern University Press, 2001.

P. 032 Yourcenar, Marguerite. "Introduction." The Writing of Stones by Roger Caillois. Translated by Barbara Bray. Charlottesville: University Press of Virginia, 1985.

P. 038 Newsom, Joanna. "Emily." Ys. Drag City, 2006.

P. 040 *The Wagner Garden* Carpet, central Iran, early 17th century, the Burrell Collection, Glasgow. Photo from the Museum of Fine Arts, Houston, www.houstonpress.com/arts/things-to-do-count-the-predators-and-prey-in-the-wagner-garden-carpet-at-mfah-11021226.

P. 044 Caillois, Roger. The Writing of Stones, with an Introduction by Marguerite Yourcenar. Translated by Barbara Bray. Charlottesville: University Press of Virginia, 1985.

P. 046 Lear, Jonathan. "A Note on Zeno's Arrow." *Phronesis*, vol. 26, no. 2, 1981, pp. 91-104. JSTOR, www.jstor.org/stable/4182117.

Figure 01, P. 009 Fragment of students' work on accretion at the Architectural Association, London, UK.

1. 1D8A6315 07:11 H
2. 1D8A6371 07:29 H
3. 1D8A6766 07:50 H
4. 1D8A6703 08:08 H
5. 1D8A6097 10:11 H
6. 1D8A6487 10:20 H
7. 1D8A5853 10:51 H
8. 1D8A6601 11:18 H
9. 1D8A6653 12:14 H
10. 1D8A6551 14:35 H
11. 1D8A6622 17:56 H
12. 1D8A5610 18:01 H

P. 060

Figure 02, P. 011

Aristolochia seed. Can be found among shrubs and forests along both the Pacific and Atlantic Coasts of Mexico. It was named and described in 1760 by Nikolaus Joseph von Jacquin and published in *Enumeration Systematica Plantarum, quas in insulus Caribeais*.

1. 1D8A6321 07:20 H
2. 1D8A6383 07:31 H
3. 1D8A6046 09:05 H
4. 1D8A6103 09:18 H
5. 1D8A6510 09:21 H
6. 1D8A5861 09:40 H
7. 1D8A6600 10:07 H
8. 1D8A6545 10:33 H
9. 1D8A5925 10:51 H
10. 1D8A6161 11:14 H
11. 1D8A5979 15:26 H
12. 1D8A6720 18:02 H

P. 062

Figure 03, P. 013

Fordite, composed of hardened layers of automotive paint from hand-operated spray guns.
Detroit, USA.

1. 1D8A6316 07:03 H
2. 1D8A6374 07:25 H
3. 1D8A6674 09:00 H
4. 1D8A6040 09:30 H
5. 1D8A6495 10:00 H
6. 1D8A6099 10:30 H
7. 1D8A6857 10:54 H
8. 1D8A6155 14:45 H
9. 1D8A5920 15:24 H
10. 1D8A6529 17:30 H
11. 1D8A6602 17:43 H
12. 1D8A6719 18:02 H

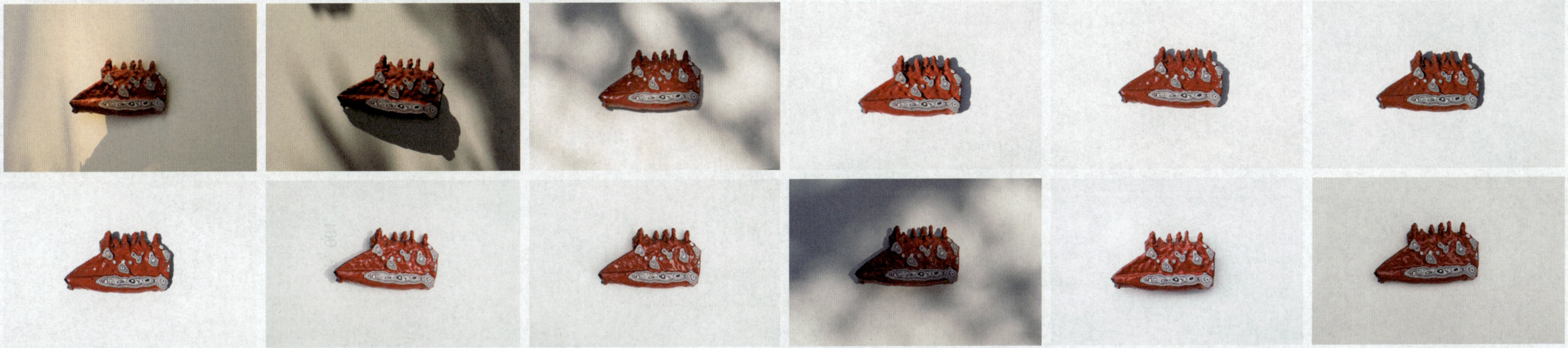

P. 064

Figure 04, P. 015

Scallop shell from Manaure, Colombia. Taken from the vicinity of Manaure Salt Flats. Closeby is Cerrajón, one of the largest open-air coal mines in the world, and La Pista, a former airport runway in Maicao that is now one of the largest refugee camps in Latin America and home for over 2000 families that fled from Venezuela. Nearby lies a plane track that functions as a refugee camp for Venezuelan migrants.

1. 1D8A6756 07:12 H
2. 1D8A6317 07:25 H
3. 1D8A6774 07:38 H
4. 1D8A6039 09:12 H
5. 1D8A6098 10:06 H
6. 1D8A6493 10:15 H
7. 1D8A5854 10:37 H
8. 1D8A6671 10:44 H
9. 1D8A6526 10:52 H
10. 1D8A5919 14:45 H
11. 1D8A5154 14:45 H
12. 1D8A6718 15:24 H

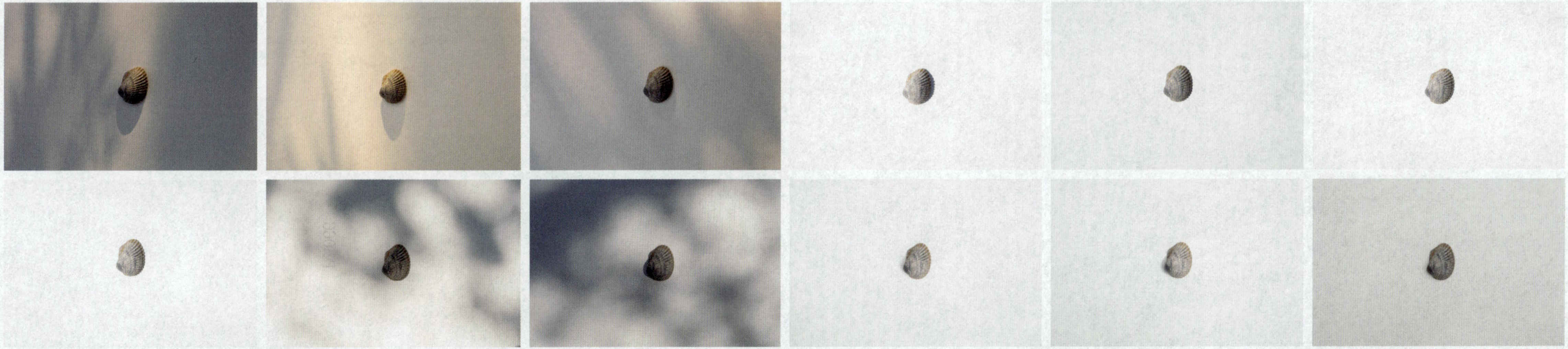

P. 066

Figure 05, P. 017

Pebbles collected at Chapultepec Park that hold traces of a Francis Alÿs performance from his exhibition *A Story of Negotiation*, at Museo Tamayo Arte Contemporáneo.

1. 1D8A6759 07:26 H
2. 1D8A6776 07:29 H
3. 1D8A6415 07:40 H
4. 1D8A6683 08:47 H
5. 1D8A6352 10:00 H
6. 1D8A6513 10:27 H
7. 1D8A6819 10:50 H
8. 1D8A6297 11:00 H
9. 1D8A6655 15:28 H
10. 1D8A6617 17:50 H
11. 1D8A6549 18:00 H
12. 1D8A6724 18:30 H

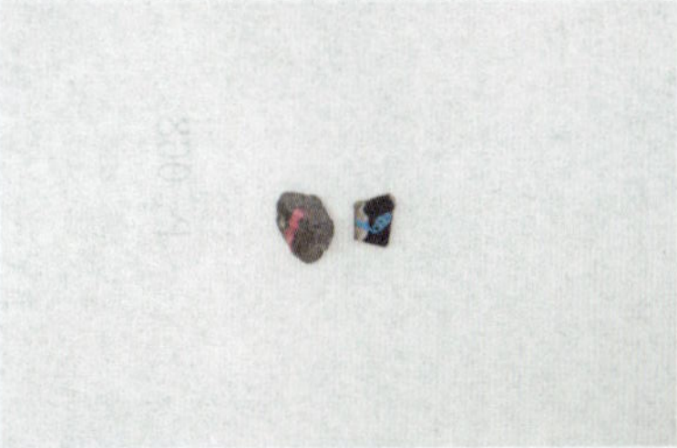

P. 068

Figure 06, P. 019

Sand from the Ordos desert in China, where a 100-villa project, Ordos 100, was never built.

1. 1D8A6772 07:00 H
2. 1D8A6320 07:13 H
3. 1D8A6773 07:35 H
4. 1D8A6382 08:00 H
5. 1D8A6706 09:16 H
6. 1D8A6489 09:30 H
7. 1D8A6856 10:12 H
8. 1D8A6821 10:28 H
9. 1D8A6657 10:34 H
10. 1D8A6830 11:00 H
11. 1D8A6520 11:19 H
12. 1D8A6809 18:12 H

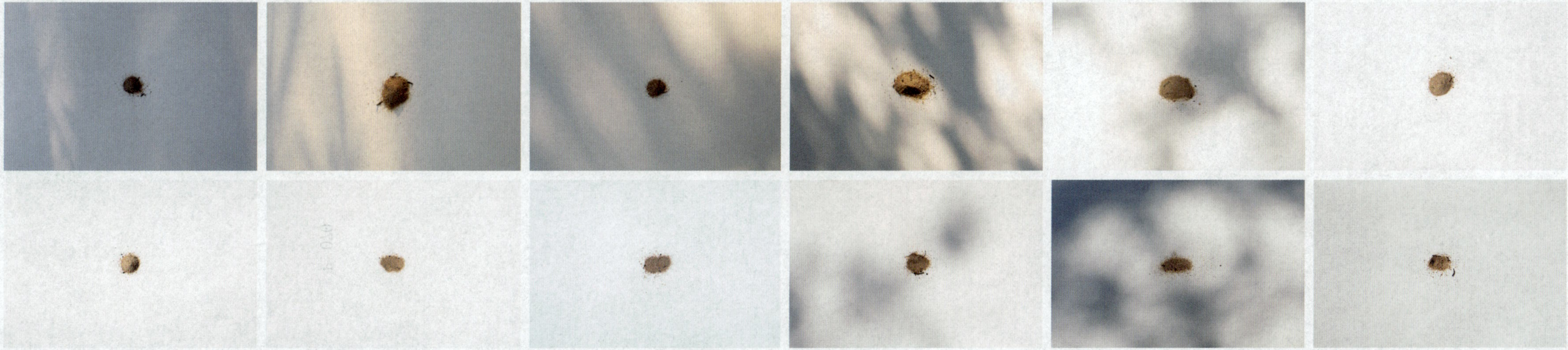

Figure 07, P. 021

Colorless calcite. Because of its clear nature and occassional brown hues, this mineral was used for optical purposes in antiquity. It is thought to have been used by Viking navigators as a “sunstone.”

1. 1D8A6761 07:21 H
2. 1D8A6777 07:27 H
3. 1D8A6337 07:40 H
4. 1D8A6399 08:38 H
5. 1D8A6685 10:18 H
6. 1D8A6612 10:41 H
7. 1D8A6126 11:00 H
8. 1D8A6182 14:46 H
9. 1D8A6536 15:00 H
10. 1D8A5963 15:29 H
11. 1D8A6029 17:40 H
12. 1D8A6640 18:00 H

P. 072

Figure 08, P. 023

Found on the seemingly virgin shores of Miyako Beach in Japan, after the inauguration of a community center designed by Kasuyo. The 2011 Tōhoku tsunami had devastated the region. These are, presumably, remains of porcelain tableware, coming from the houses that had bordered the beach a few months earlier.

1. 1D8A6332 07:18 H
2. 1D8A5812 08:21 H
3. 1D8A6389 09:08 H
4. 1D8A6666 10:11 H
5. 1D8A6491 10:25 H
6. 1D8A6109 10:30 H
7. 1D8A6053 10:45 H
8. 1D8A5868 11:30 H
9. 1D8A5988 15:19 H
10. 1D8A6521 15:42 H
11. 1D8A6713 17:01 H
12. 1D8A6636 17:02 H

Figure 09, P. 025 Magnolia flower from our mother's house in Chimalistac, Mexico City.

1. 1D8A6834 07:24 H
2. 1D8A6831 07:54 H
3. 1D8A6854 08:02 H
4. 1D8A6851 09:12 H
5. 1D8A6845 09:20 H
6. 1D8A6782 09:23 H
7. 1D8A6853 10:30 H
8. 1D8A6799 10:39 H
9. 1D8A6787 10:45 H
10. 1D8A6823 10:50 H
11. 1D8A6734 11:00 H
12. 1D8A6847 11:30 H

Figure 10, P. 027 Dandelion-in-resin paperweigh.

1. 1D8A6325 07:15 H
2. 1D8A6384 08:19 H
3. 1D8A6677 08:47 H
4. 1D8A6860 09:14 H
5. 1D8A6047 10:00 H
6. 1D8A6104 10:04 H
7. 1D8A6496 10:25 H
8. 1D8A5862 10:39 H
9. 1D8A6632 11:02 H
10. 1D8A5927 15:09 H
11. 1D8A6531 17:52 H
12. 1D8A6162 18:31 H

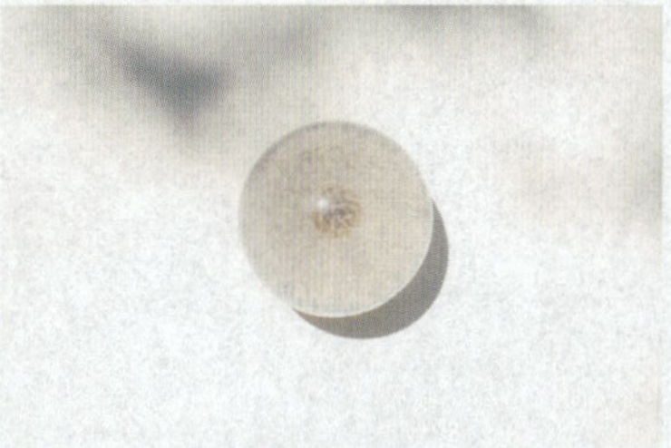

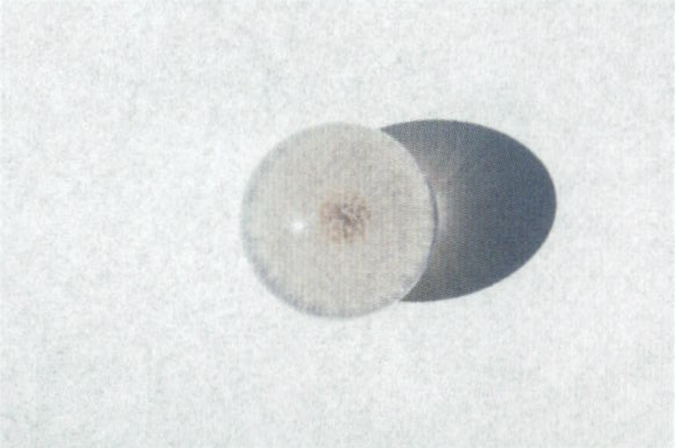
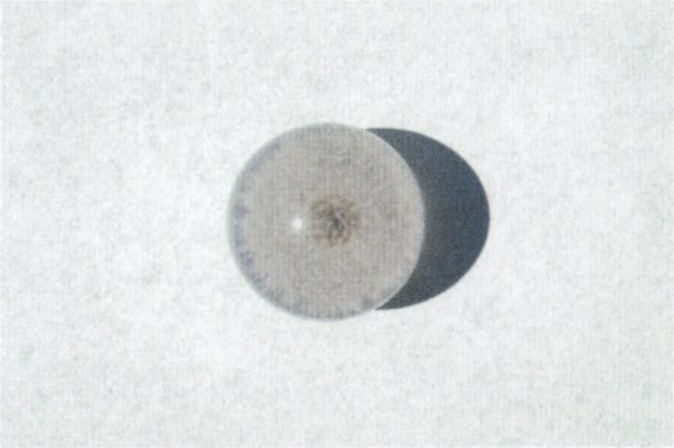
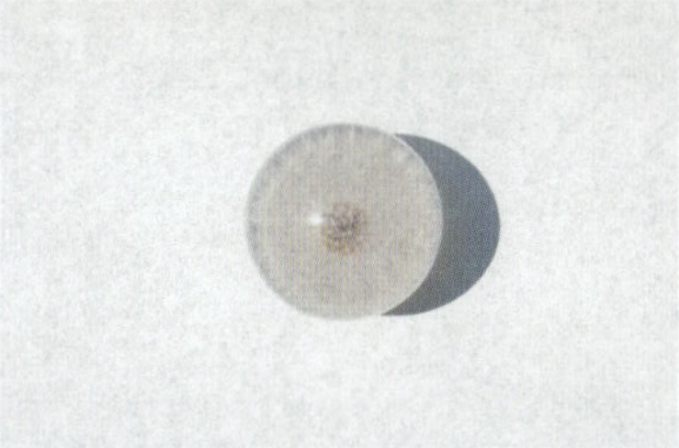
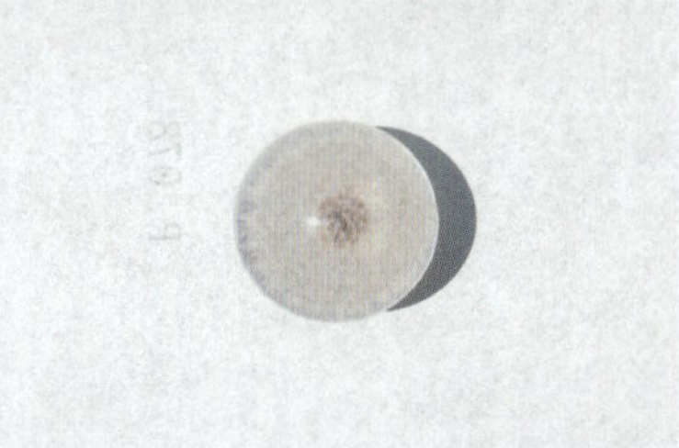
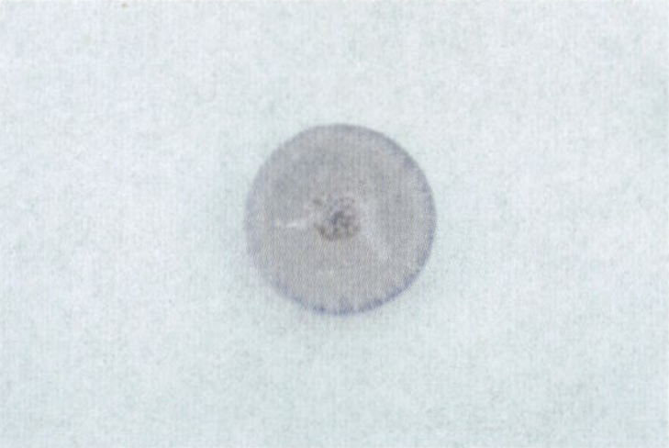

Figure 11, P. 029

Chestnut seeds collected at the Kensington Gardens on the day of the closure of the Serpentine Pavilion 2018.

1. 1D8A6762 07:28 H
2. 1D8A6801 08:02 H
3. 1D8A6800 08:30 H
4. 1D8A6840 08:55 H
5. 1D8A6843 09:05 H
6. 1D8A6810 09:16 H
7. 1D8A6052 10:26 H
8. 1D8A6108 10:34 H
9. 1D8A6818 10:51 H
10. 1D8A5867 11:00 H
11. 1D8A5987 11:30 H
12. 1D8A6168 14:22 H

P. 080

Figure 12, P. 031

Oud collected during a trip to Dubai. Known as the “wood of the gods” it is the basis of some of the world’s most extravagant perfumes. It is derived from the resinous bark of a wild tropical tree called Agar, which grows exclusively in certain parts of Southeast Asia. Since only 2% of Agar trees produce Oud, it is considered one of the world’s rarest and most precious commodities.

1. 1D8A6334 07:19 H
2. 1D8A6395 08:36 H
3. 1D8A6693 09:18 H
4. 1D8A6057 09:51 H
5. 1D8A6505 11:10 H
6. 1D8A5653 12:45 H
7. 1D8A5994 14:42 H
8. 1D8A6637 15:30 H
9. 1D8A6173 18:03 H
10. 1D8A6296 18:30 H
11. 1D8A6539 12:47 H
12. 1D8A6731 14:17 H

Figure 13, P. 033 Pink Rhyolite from the Popocatépetl's volcanic eruption.

1. 1D8A6412 08:46 H
2. 1D8A6064 09:20 H
3. 1D8A6133 10:03 H
4. 1D8A6506 10:19 H
5. 1D8A5897 10:50 H
6. 1D8A5944 11:21 H
7. 1D8A6540 14:50 H
8. 1D8A6752 15:31 H
9. 1D8A6190 16:00 H
10. 1D8A6751 17:40 H
11. 1D8A6618 18:00 H
12. 1D8A6619 18:20 H

Figure 14, P. 035 Snout beetle from the Eastern Mediterranean Sea encapsulated in marble-sized resin.

1. 1D8A6392 07:42 H
2. 1D8A6670 09:19 H
3. 1D8A6058 10:12 H
4. 1D8A6112 10:30 H
5. 1D8A6492 10:45 H
6. 1D8A5872 10:56 H
7. 1D8A6651 11:00 H
8. 1D8A5995 14:53 H
9. 1D8A6525 15:23 H
10. 1D8A5937 15:26 H
11. 1D8A6716 18:00 H
12. 1D8A6174 18:09 H

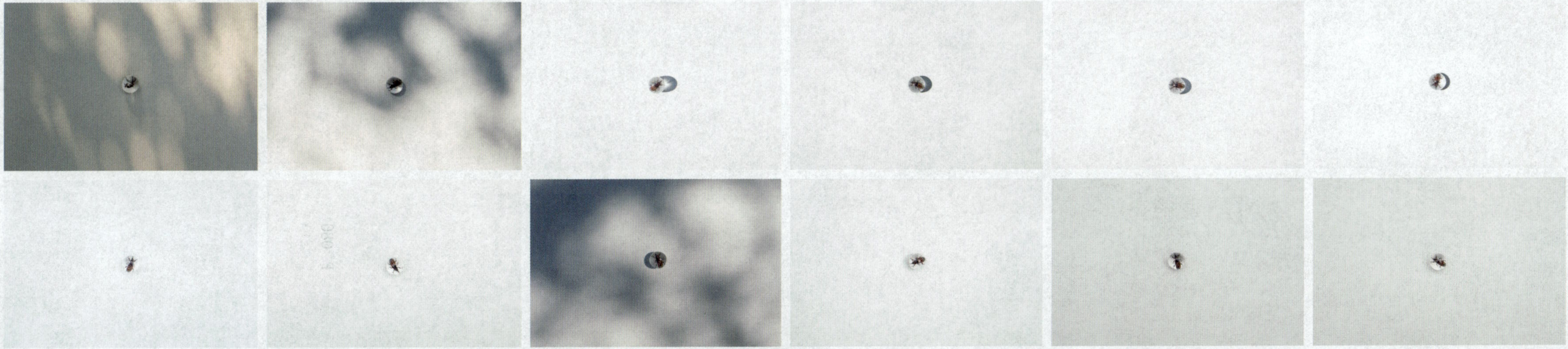

Figure 15, P. 037 Pyrite sun from Illinois, USA, nearly 350 million years old.

1. 1D8A6336 07:20 H
2. 1D8A6398 08:37 H
3. 1D8A6682 09:34 H
4. 1D8A6087 10:19 H
5. 1D8A6610 10:40 H
6. 1D8A6498 11:05 H
7. 1D8A6125 11:23 H
8. 1D8A5893 14:47 H
9. 1D8A6287 14:47 H
10. 1D8A6642 17:56 H
11. 1D8A6185 18:51 H
12. 1D8A6533 18:05 H

P. 088

Figure 16, P. 039 Molten lead found in Greenpoint, NYC.

1. 1D8A6353 07:28 H
2. 1D8A6416 08:52 H
3. 1D8A6673 09:26 H
4. 1D8A6071 10:15 H
5. 1D8A6494 10:23 H
6. 1D8A6141 10:38 H
7. 1D8A5904 10:53 H
8. 1D8A6306 11:24 H
9. 1D8A6528 14:53 H
10. 1D8A6717 15:23 H
11. 1D8A6195 19:00 H
12. 1D8A6626 18:00 H

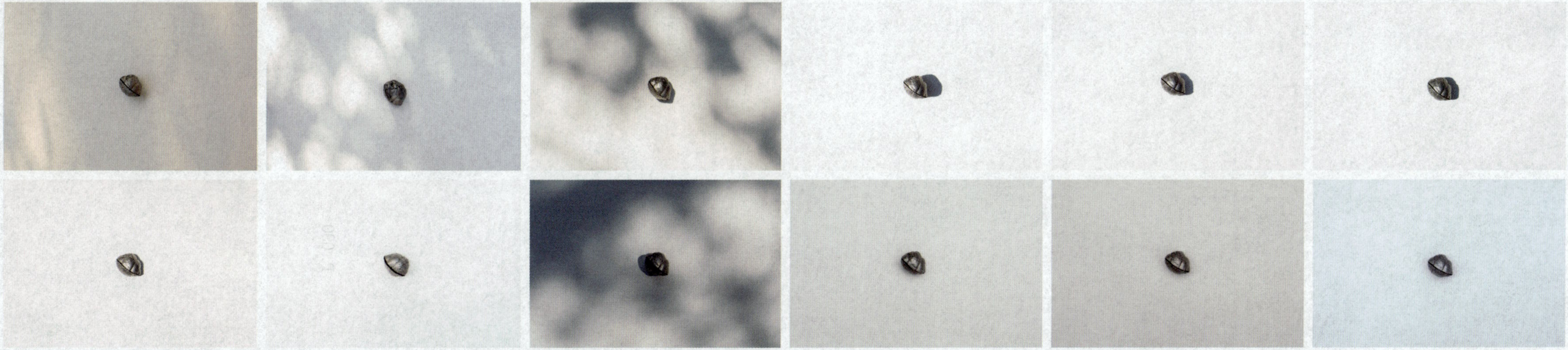

P. 090

Figure 17, P. 041

Miniature replica of a panel of the bronze doors at the Basilica of San Zeno, Verona, Italy.

1. 1D8A6329 07:17 H
2. 1D8A6386 08:19 H
3. 1D8A6690 09:14 H
4. 1D8A6049 10:09 H
5. 1D8A6105 10:20 H
6. 1D8A6504 10:42 H
7. 1D8A5863 10:49 H
8. 1D8A5928 11:00 H
9. 1D8A6273 14:48 H
10. 1D8A6608 15:00 H
11. 1D8A6163 18:30 H
12. 1D8A6538 17:53 H

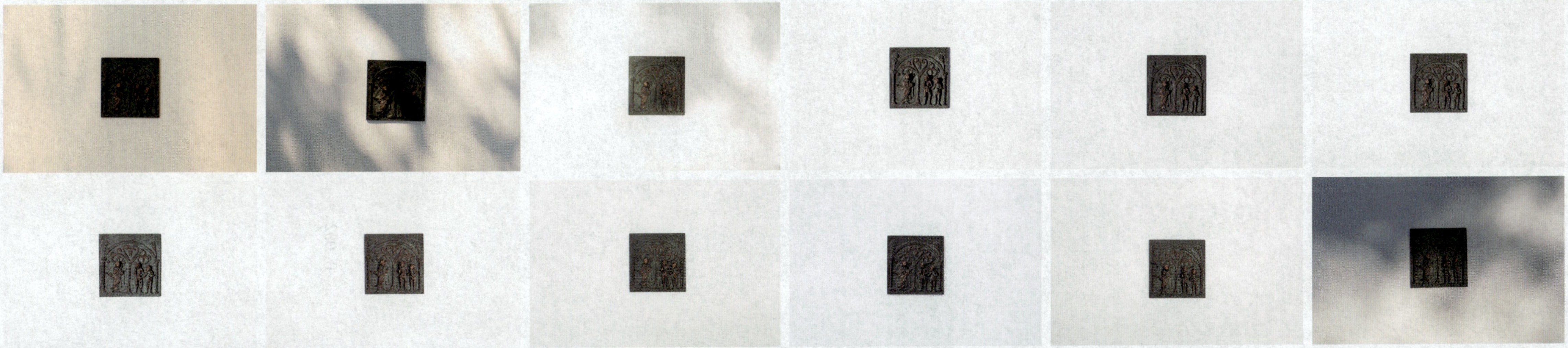

P. 092

Figure 18, P. 043

Diagnostic doll, used by women in China to signal their ailments to doctors at a time when pointing to or describing their own bodies was deemed improper.

1. 1D8A6679 07:17 H
2. 1D8A6060 08:19 H
3. 1D8A6115 09:14 H
4. 1D8A6497 10:09 H
5. 1D8A5874 10:20 H
6. 1D8A6280 10:42 H
7. 1D8A5998 10:49 H
8. 1D8A5939 11:00 H
9. 1D8A6604 14:48 H
10. 1D8A6628 15:00 H
11. 1D8A6176 18:30 H
12. 1D8A6722 17:53 H

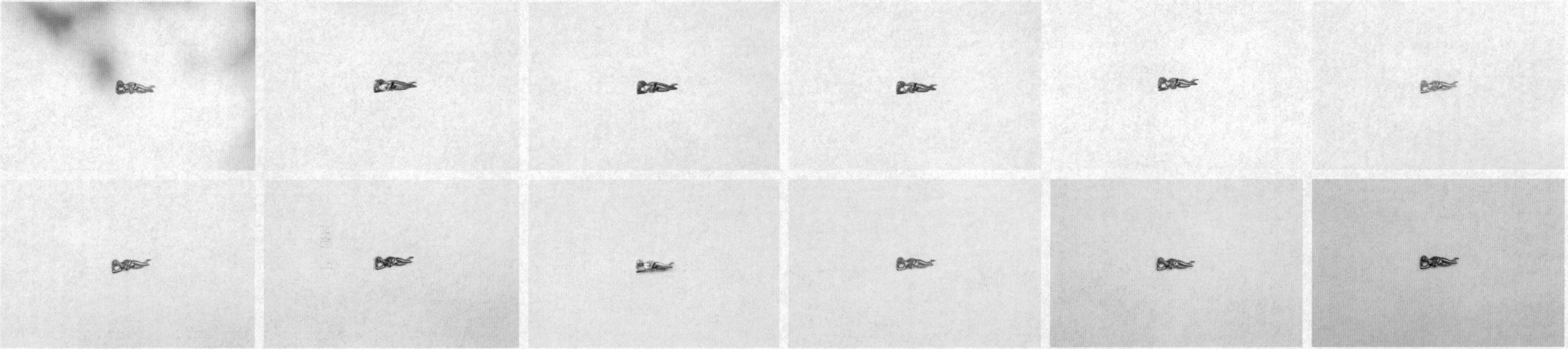

Figure 19, P. 045

This significantly pseudomorphic specimen is called Romanechite. It was found in a small fossil shop in Île Saint-Louis, Paris.

1. 1D8A6366 09:30 H
2. 1D8A6433 10:23 H
3. 1D8A6662 10:28 H
4. 1D8A6082 10.47 H
5. 1D8A6151 11:00 H
6. 1D8A6509 13:00 H
7. 1D8A5915 15:15 H
8. 1D8A6303 15:37 H
9. 1D8A6021 18:00 H
10. 1D8A6709 18:16 H
11. 1D8A6546 18:35 H
12. 1D8A6659 18:59 H

P. 096

Figure 20, P. 047

Pre-Columbian obsidian arrowhead, a gift from the late Juan Fraga, a magnificent stone artist from Mexico City.

1. 1D8A5813 07:16 H　2. 1D8A6327 09:15 H　3. 1D8A6699 10:10 H　4. 1D8A6050 10:24 H　5. 1D8A6106 14:00 H　6. 1D8A6511 14:39 H

7. 1D8A5865 14:48 H　8. 1D8A5929 17:01 H　9. 1D8A6165 17:30 H　10. 1D8A6274 17:53 H　11. 1D8A6609 16:01 H　12. 1D8A6630 17:26 H

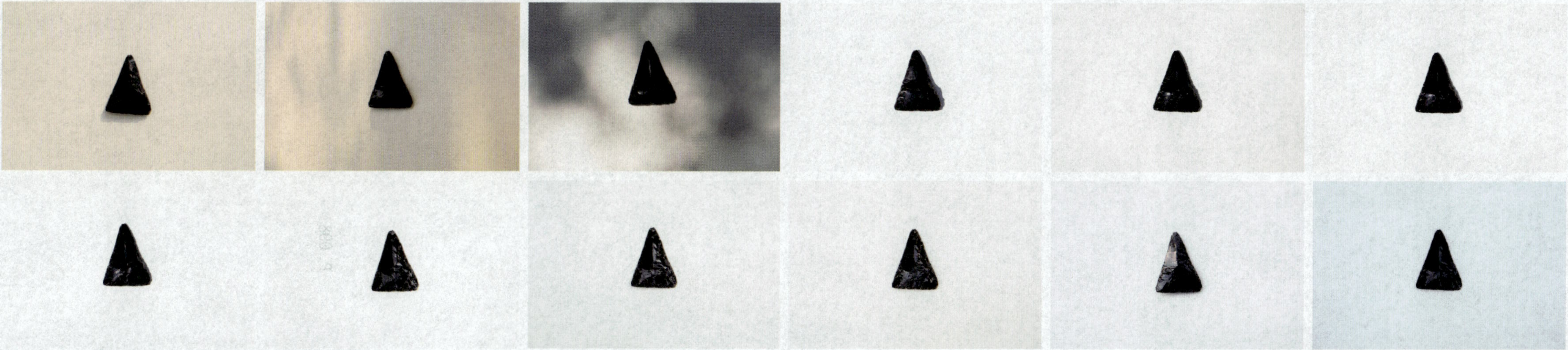

Figure 21, P. 049 Coral from Vieques, Puerto Rico.

1. 1D8A6403 07:23 H
2. 1D8A6341 07:29 H
3. 1D8A6702 10:16 H
4. 1D8A6764 10:20 H
5. 1D8A6122 10:35 H
6. 1D8A6820 11:00 H
7. 1D8A6512 11:27 H
8. 1D8A5892 11:31 H
9. 1D8A6289 12:01 H
10. 1D8A6548 13:21 H
11. 1D8A5964 14:15 H
12. 1D8A6614 18:07 H

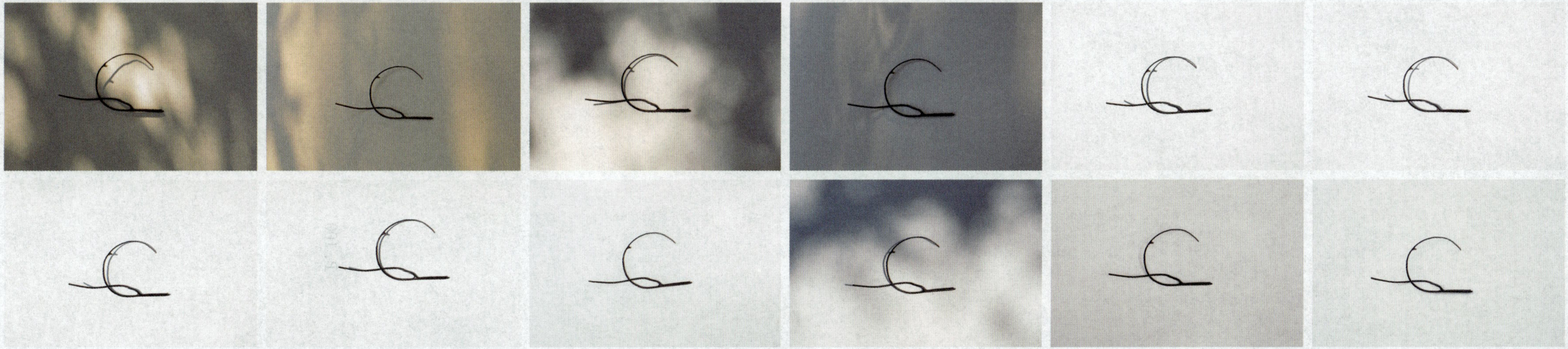

P. 100

Figure 22, P. 051 Miniature box from Kyoto, Japan.

1. 1D8A6333 07:19 H
2. 1D8A6331 09:17 H
3. 1D8A6667 10:12 H
4. 1D8A6817 10:30 H
5. 1D8A6055 11:00 H
6. 1D8A6111 11:30 H
7. 1D8A5869 12:03 H
8. 1D8A5989 13:24 H
9. 1D8A5935 14:41 H
10. 1D8A6171 14:51 H
11. 1D8A6284 18:00 H
12. 1D8A6714 18:30 H

Figure 23, P. 053

Empty capsule taken from Carsten Holler's "Pill Clock" at the New Museum, New York, USA. 2011.

P. 102

1. 1D8A6770 07:23 H
2. 1D8A6343 07:33 H
3. 1D8A6408 07:56 H
4. 1D8A6409 08:15 H
5. 1D8A6789 08:43 H
6. 1D8A6794 08:50 H
7. 1D8A6550 10:28 H
8. 1D8A6661 10:47 H
9. 1D8A6514 10:50 H
10. 1D8A6656 15:14 H
11. 1D8A6708 18:45 H
12. 1D8A6293 18:53 H

P. 104

Figure 24, P. 055

Luminescent mineral. This specimen absorbs visible light and releases some of its energy in small amounts, glowing even minutes after the light source is gone.

1. 1D8A6757 08:00 H
2. 1D8A6346 08:21 H
3. 1D8A6407 08:42 H
4. 1D8A6705 09.36 H
5. 1D8A6519 10:11 H
6. 1D8A6859 10:43 H
7. 1D8A6091 15:11 H
8. 1D8A6488 17:25 H
9. 1D8A6615 17:58 H
10. 1D8A6749 19:00 H
11. 1D8A6747 19:30 H
12. 1D8A6748 22:00 H

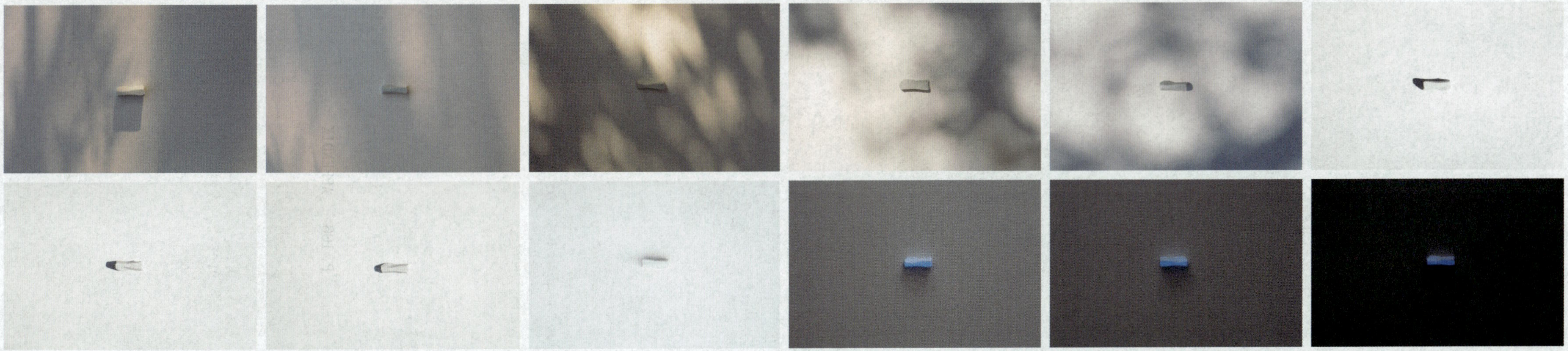

P. 106 APPENDIX